THE
Teddy Bear
Lover's

Companion

BEING A BOOK OF THEIR
LIFE AND TIMES

Ted Menten

Acropolis Books

Acknowledgments

I wish to express my thanks to the following people:
The entire staff at Running Press, who are not only
professional, but very calm and who make being an author
a real pleasure.
Barbara Wolters and "Dumper," whose original thoughts
about traveling teddies helped to make that chapter a
success.
Bob Smith, for taking my picture and managing not to
make me look as old as I feel.
Diane Gard, for her enduring friendship and faith in
this project . . . a great big hug.
And finally, to all the bears and their talented creators,
without whom this book would not have been possible.

♥

First published in Great Britain in 1992 by
Acropolis Books
Bookmart Ltd
Desford Road, Enderby
Leicestershire LE9 5AD
United Kingdom

First published in the United States by
Running Press Book Publishers
125 South Twenty-second Street
Philadelphia, Pennsylvania 19103

A CIP catalogue record for this book is available from the British
Library

Interior design and photographs by Ted Menten.

ISBN 1-873762-40-2

Contents

♥

Grumpy Ed: A Remembrance

In the early days, when I started collecting teddy bears, my friend Ed joined me on a number of teddy bear hunts. At the time, he was not a collector, but in the years that followed, Ed, too, gave in to the charm of teddy bears and began a collection of his own. He admired the originality and craftsmanship of the hand-made, artist bears and his bear den grew to fill the rooms of his little house that sat high on a hill in San Francisco.

Ed was a talented stained-glass artist as well as a painter and woodworker. He wrote many wonderful books about stained glass, including one with teddy bear designs. He loved sitting in his bay window, surrounded by his teddy bears and glass pieces, looking at the children playing in the grassy park across from his house. Twice a day, Ed and his little dachshund, Frodo, would cross the street and romp on the grassy slopes of the park.

When Ed became ill and learned that his condition was terminal, he devoted the last years of his life to helping others who, like himself, were facing impending death. Now that he's gone, his teddy bear companions reside with friends and family, serving as gentle reminders of Ed.

What follows is the story which I first set down in *The TeddyBear Lovers Catalog* in 1983. It is just one of many wonderful memories of my friend, but it is one of my favorites.

While doing research for this book in California, I was caught in the advanced grip of shopper's fever, attempting to buy out *The Ready Teddy,* one bear at a time—very quickly. The counter was stacked high with bears and the young lady behind the counter seemed to be taking the whole thing in her stride. Obviously she'd seen a bear nut before.

My best friend and fellow author, Ed Sibbett, was along for the ride, so to speak. Ed is a patient sort who endures my madness with a quiet smile of amusement. He is immune to shopper's fever and can actually browse.

As I frantically grabbed up bears, ostensibly to photograph for this book, Ed browsed.

On the shelf sat a grayish long-haired bear with quite a grumpy expression. Ed picked him up and asked if I liked him. I didn't, because I wanted smiling bears for the book. Ed persisted that he thought this bear had presence. I replied that he liked the bear because it was grumpy, like him.

Now Ed isn't really grumpy except if you accuse him of it . . .then he gets grumpy. Well, this bear became something of an issue, with the result that Ed left the store and I had to carry all the bears home by myself.

It didn't end there. Ed insisted that the bear had liked me and was disappointed that I had left him behind. I replied that I still thought he was a grumpy-looking bear and that he would likely find a very nice home somewhere; and if Ed was so worried about the bear, why didn't he adopt him?

It didn't end there. Christmas came, and sitting under the tree was a large box, elaborately wrapped, festooned with ribbons and punctured with air holes!

You guessed it! Inside was the grumpy bear bearing embossed army dog tags that read:

GRUMPY ED LOVES YOU

And if that doesn't tug at your heartstrings, nothing will.

♥

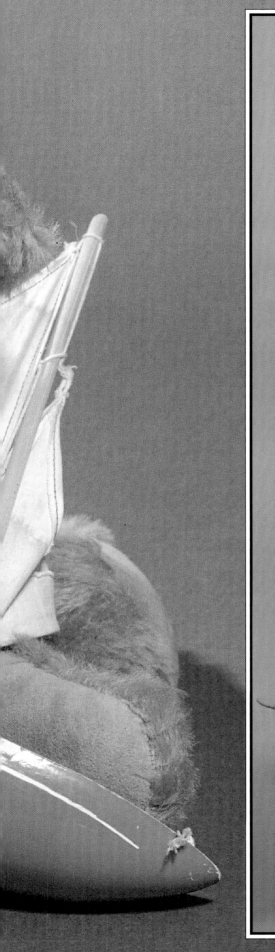

Looking Back

Sitting in a Victorian rocking chair, gazing out at the New York City skyline through a rain-streaked window, I am irresistibly drawn back to my childhood by memories that seem too vivid to really be from so long ago. My cat, Kapusta, jumps into my lap, nuzzles me for attention and brings me back into the present. I look about the room into the bright, glistening eyes of the teddy bears sitting on every available surface, and I chuckle to myself and wonder how it all began.

Wouldn't it be helpful if we could know in advance how our lives were intended to progress? It might be equally helpful if we could plan the events of our lives in some series of logical steps. However, it has been my experience that that kind of vision and planning is simply not available. While it's true that parents and friends and the high-school guidance counselor are all very helpful in pointing out various directions on life's highway, there's no road that leads directly to a destination called "teddy bear artist."

I suspect that like every other teddy bear artist, I stumbled into it by fortunate accident. One might say that I fell into it backwards.

You may know what they say about Geminis: they have split personalities. That's true, we do. My two different sides are called, "with my tie on" and "with my tie off." These are my dual natures: serious and capricious.

My childhood was spent in a whimsical family circle that included my somewhat zany grandmother who collected dolls and stuffed animals. My father designed and built scale-model railroad trains and had constructed a miniature world for them in the basement of our house. I was enlisted to glue tiny pieces of sponge to tree twigs and paint them green for landscaping. My mother collected tiny china cats from around the world.

Our neighbors were professional puppeteers, and at age ten they taught me to carve, sew, and perform with hand puppets and marionettes. In those early days of my childhood almost everyone we knew was artistic, and no one wore ties.

Between making sponge trees for my father and learning to properly joint a marionette, I struggled to have a normal childhood. I envied my friends with their stout mothers who spent hours in the kitchen baking cookies and who seemed to always have a bit of flour on one cheek. I yearned for a father who worked at an office and wore a tie. Such was not to be my fate. Today I am grateful, but back then it didn't seem so wonderful.

I graduated from school, learned to wear a tie, and did serious work for years and years. I understood the work ethic as it was explained to me by a man in a tie.

For many years I was a serious, tie-wearing designer who designed packaging for serious products like perfume and deodorant. If you doubt the seriousness of these products, you should eavesdrop on a board meeting at one of these companies (where everyone wears a tie) and listen to the board solemnly plot the destiny of underarms for the next decade. Believe me —there's no room for levity at these meetings. That's serious stuff?

It wasn't long before I began to feel strangled by my tie, so I decided to hang it up and cultivate my capriciousness. I started designing toys.

My first teddy bear designs were for a company that manufactured stuffed toys for carnivals—big pink and blue bears that were the prizes teenage boys won for their steady girls by knocking over wooden milk bottles with a baseball.

But guess what—that was serious business too. Lots of neckties. Far from being fanciful or even fun, these designs had more to do with engineering than with design, as I struggled to make all the pattern pieces fit economically on the pink fabric. Most of my finished bears looked like socks with arms and legs.

Meanwhile, I continued to live among teddy bears, but like any normal, tie-wearing type, I kept that sort of thing to myself. I struggled up the corporate ladder until I reached the top—then I jumped off. After 20 years I left the corporate world due to a persistent sense of whimsy. When I read Peter Bull's delightful classic, *The Teddy Bear Book,* I brought a few of my bears out of the closet and began openly cavorting with them. Then I attended the first Teddy Tribune Convention, and I found myself surrounded by hundreds of fellow teddy bear lovers.

But I was still struggling with standard ideas of business and success, and although I had taken to wearing a tie with teddy bears on it, it was still a tie and I still

wasn't having any fun.

Several years ago I was at a teddy bear banquet, sitting at the head table in front of all those friendly, smiling arctophiles who had invited me to be their guest speaker. This, of course, was very pleasant—even fun. It was also to be a turning point in my life, precipitated by—of all things—the lowly brussels sprout.

When I was a child, my grandmother had always told me that if I ate my brussels sprouts, the good fairy would reward me. Frankly, there was no reward great enough on the face of the earth to coax me into putting a brussels sprout into my mouth. I squeamishly passed on the offer. Mystical rewards from vegetable fairies aside, my mother had always, *always* said that it was rude not to eat everything on your plate if you were a guest.

At this teddy bear banquet, I was served, among other things, a rather sizeable portion of my least favorite vegetable. And, mainly out of respect for my mother, I ate every last sprout. While it wasn't the worst thing that has ever happened to me, it was close, *very close.*

But lo and behold: the brussels sprout fairy delivered, rewarding me with a brand-new, sparkling insight!

Not long after the banquet, I was commissioned to create a line of teddy bear kits. In past commercial projects, an assistant had always done all the sewing, but I decided that in the interest of writing clear, workable instructions, I should try to make one bear all by myself. In the end, I had made all ten of them and loved every minute of the process. Since then, I have not stopped making teddy bears, and each day is happier than the one before, as each new bear comes to life and makes me smile to myself. There are lots of rewards for wearing a tie and doing regular work and solving important problems such as what next year's underarm fragrance will be. But thanks to the brussels sprout fairy's gift of insight, I have discovered another kind of success—one that doesn't require a tie or fill up your bank account. It's a simple insight, but one easily forgotten in day-to-day living: Do what you like best, not what you think you're "supposed" to do. Only then will you be a success.

Now I know what success really means. For me, it's that moment when a stranger picks up a teddy bear that was born in my imagination and brought to life by my own hands—and smiles. On my ladder of success, that smile is the top rung.

The One True Bear

The first time I saw her, she was sitting in the park watching her three-year-old son playing with the other neighborhood children in a sandbox. I noticed that she was very attentive, very alert to his every action.

A few weeks later I saw them again. This time she was pushing him on the swings. He kept giggling and asking to be pushed higher. Again I noticed that she was alert to his movements and there was an edge to her voice as she instructed him to hold tightly while she pushed him still higher.

A few days later, as I was crossing the street, I saw them again. She was holding his arm and he was clutching a large teddy bear under his arm. The bear was unusually tattered and worn and I remember thinking that it had certainly had a lot of loving.

As the summer faded and the leaves turned crimson, I once again saw the young woman and her child together with the worn teddy bear. All three were wearing hand-knitted red wool scarves, and the mother was handing her son the fallen leaves and talking quietly to him. It was the first time I realized that he was blind.

As the woman held her child's finger and traced the veins of the leaf, he giggled the same giggle he had while flying high on the swing. His mother leaned over, kissed his cheek, and hugged him. As she did so, his teddy bear fell to the ground beyond his reach and he cried out, as though wounded, "Bear! Bear!" His mother retrieved the bear and the child clutched it in his arms as she had held him. The bad moment passed, and soon they were laughing again.

I love watching people with their bears. The very private relationship between a human and a teddy bear is wonderful, but not easy to explain.

How often I have watched as a child tends to the needs of his or her bear and realized that the gestures were the same as those used by adults. Is teddy bear love so universal that it spans all ages, or is it that we learn very early how to express it—even if we are blind?

I remember the first time I saw a bunch of teddy bear collectors gathered together at a convention. It was 1983 and I was working on my first book about teddy bears. I flew to Minneapolis to attend the first *Teddy Tribune* Convention, and I had no idea what to expect. The idea of grownups cavorting publicly with teddy bears was curious to me. Being six-foot-five, I tend to stand out in any crowd, and if I were to carry a teddy bear, I would surely turn heads. But everyone else was doing it, so I cast caution to the wind, and joined the party.

After awhile I began to notice that many of the bears being carried were old and worn-looking. Obviously they had been loved for many years. But a number of people carried newer bears that were favorites. These bears were dressed up like characters from their owners' fantasies, each costume holding some personal significance known only to the bears and their owners. These bears had a charm that was expressed more by how their owners saw them than by how they actually looked. All of these teddies were loved the way the little boy in the park loved his bear—blindly.

Suddenly I felt deprived—I had no special bear. As is often the case with the overindulged, I had too many bears right from the beginning, starting from my crib days. As a result, I had neither the need nor the opportunity to form a relationship with one special bear.

After the convention, I continued to add new bears to my collection. It wasn't long before my den of bears overflowed from one room to another, I had to rent a storeroom for my other things. I had hundreds of dolls and various antiques of every size and description. In order to make room for all my bears, I had to unpack and reorganize boxes that I hadn't opened in years. One box contained mementos from my childhood. There, nestled among the comic books, tin soldiers, puppets, high-school yearbooks and fading snapshots, was a teddy bear.

He wasn't my first crib bear; he wasn't even a bear from my childhood. He was the first bear I had

bought for myself when I was twelve. The first thing I did was smell him, because I remembered liking the straw smell that came from his stuffing. Amazingly, the fragrance was still there after all those years. He was in good shape except for one missing eye, and so I took him to the local doll hospital and had him fitted for a new eye.

Back home again, I sat gazing at this bear and he gazed back at me through bright new eyes. My mind wandered back to that simpler time when we were both much younger. Suddenly, I was overcome by a rush of memories—images so vivid that they seemed to have happened only yesterday.

I asked myself, does maturity mean abandoning our beloved teddy bears, and truest childhood friends, or does it mean being strong enough to proudly proclaim our devotion to them? If I had to choose, there would be no contest—the kind of maturity that has no room for whimsy is meaningless and offers no reward. Give me the warmth of a tattered teddy any day.

♥

The Answer Bear

The world of teddy bears and their companions is filled with strange customs and unfamiliar terminology. The casual visitor or novice collector may step back, slightly bewildered, after hearing that, "An arctophile has just adopted a very fine fully-jointed, mohair Steiff with shoe-button eyes." What sort of strange creature is an arctophile, and what sort of *thing* has it adopted?

In an effort to make this visit to the world of teddy bears and their human companions more comfortable, and therefore more enjoyable, The Answer Bear has volunteered to respond to a few questions, dispel a myth or two, and shed a little light on the subject.

Q: What is an *arctophile*?
A human who enjoys the company of teddy bears and carries at least one as a constant companion is called an arctophile or arctophilist (arc-TUFF-ill-ist).

Q: Why are stuffed bears called Teddy?
The first stuffed toy bears were replicas of real bears and made of fabric and stuffing just like any other toy dog or cat or rabbit. In 1902, President Theodore Roosevelt was the subject of a political cartoon (see page 41) which depicted the president refusing to shoot a bear cub. The popularity of the president and his little bear, which appeared in all the subsequent cartoons about the president, finally led to the term *Teddy's Bear,* which was later shortened to teddy bear. While there is no question that the teddy bear is an American folk hero, he is extremely popular in England, where the nickname *Teddy* is used for gentlemen whose name is Edward.

Three of the most famous teddy bears in children's literature are English. The most famous in America is Winnie-the-Pooh, followed by Paddington Bear, and the long-running British comic-strip character, Rupert.

Q: What is mohair?
The first teddy bears were made of an expensive fabric made from goat hair woven to resemble fur.

This fabric is called mohair. In 1903, a short-haired version of this fabric was used to upholster fine furniture. Even today a kind of mohair is still available for seat coverings.

By 1907, the demand for teddy bears was so tremendous that fabric mills worked overtime to meet the demand. As toy manufacturers cornered the mohair market, the furniture industry faced shortages it had never known before.

During World War II, mohair was unavailable, and toy bears were made of other fabrics. After the war, synthetic fur fabrics, called *plush,* were developed, and the use of mohair became limited.

Today, mohair is still used by European and American toy manufacturers, but only for the more expensive bears. American teddy bear artists also use mohair for their gallery-quality bears. In recent years, newer, softer synthetic fibers, as well as new processes which alter the appearance of mohair, have created a greater range of fabrics for artists and manufacturers to choose from.

Q: What does the term *fully-jointed* mean?

The terms *fully-jointed* and *unjointed* refer to how the head, arms, and legs of a toy bear are attached to his body. An unjointed bear's head, arms, and legs are sewn to his body. The limbs and head of a fully-jointed bear are attached to his body with flat, wooden or plastic flat disc joints held together by cotter-pins, rivets or nuts and bolts. These joints enable the head, arms, and legs of the bear to be moved.

Q: What are shoe-button eyes?

In 1903 shoes had buttons rather than laces. The small buttons were leather-covered spheres with wire loops on the back that were sewn to the shoe. These buttons were perfect for sewing into a toy bear's face for eyes. Shoe-buttons are still to be found in antique shops and flea markets, but they are rare.

Today, artist-made teddy bears have glass versions of shoe-button eyes as well as colored glass eyes with black pupils. Commercial teddy bears have plastic "safety-eyes" which are held onto the fur with metal lock-washers preventing the eyes from being pulled out and swallowed by children.

Sewn-on eyes are still used by teddy bear artists who make bears for collectors rather than for children.

Q: What is a Steiff?

The German toy company that introduced the toy

bear, in 1902, is named Steiff (see page 42). Its toys have a small, gold-colored button imprinted with its trademark riveted to each toy's ear. The Steiff company continues to manufacture toy animals, including teddy bears, which are considered by many collectors to be the finest in the world.

Q: What is a yes-no teddy bear?
Teddy bear manufacturers have been creating specialized mechanical teddies right from the beginning. There were bears with eyes that lit up, bears that chewed things, and bears whose heads came off to reveal a perfume bottle hidden inside their tummies.
One of the most popular mechanical bears was the yes-no bear. A mechanism within the bear enabled his human companion to move the bear's head up and down or side-to-side simply by wiggling the bear's tail in the appropriate direction.

Q: What is a growler?
Every teddy bear *speaks* to the one who loves him, but some bears have a public voice called a *growler*. This voice is produced by a mechanism that is placed inside the bear's tummy and which emits a growling noise when the teddy is turned upside down. It seems to me that anyone would growl after being turned topsy-turvy.

Q: Why are teddy bears still so popular after all these years?
There are many answers to that question. Personally, I think the best answer is exactly the one you might find to an even older question: Why is love still so popular after all these years?

♥

The Legend of the Teddy Bear

A small child sits clutching a ragged and worn teddy bear that has one eye missing and patches on its paws. An old gentleman, his once-proud body humbled by age, shuffles along a hospital corridor, nervously stroking a tiny teddy bear hidden in the pocket of his bathrobe. Standing impatiently in front of an elevator is a middle-aged couple, their arms filled with brightly colored gifts, including a large, wide-eyed teddy bear who is about to become the companion of their new grandchild.

For generations, the teddy bear has been the symbol of love and comfort for millions of children and adults around the world. No other toy, except perhaps the rubber ball, has endured for so long in essentially its original form.

As with all legends, the story of the teddy bear is full of twists and turns of fate, forgotten facts and misinformation. The real story is simple.

When President Theodore Roosevelt decided to go on a well-earned vacation in November of 1902, he was at the height of his popularity as president. Hardworking and dedicated, Roosevelt was the epitome of a soldier-statesman. His famous "big stick" policy and his powerful physical presence gave him a reputation as a man's man, while his well-known devotion to his family made him popular with wives and mothers. Journalists of the day also admired the president, and good-naturedly reported his activities.

Long before our lakes and streams became polluted and our forests and wildlife became endangered, President Roosevelt established himself as a conservationist. Although Roosevelt was an avid hunter, he loved animals and respected them. It is, in fact, his respect for animals that is the core of the teddy bear legend.

Much has been written about the actual bear hunt that took place during that November, but the one distinct fact that emerges is that the president did *not* shoot a bear. By all accounts, he was disappointed that no real opportunity presented itself: The only bear sighted was tracked down and lashed to a tree for him to shoot, but the president considered that to be unsportsmanlike and beneath his standards of behavior as a hunter and as a man.

When newspaper reports of the hunting trip revealed that the president had refused to shoot a bear, the well-known political cartoonist, Clifford Berryman, used the incident to symbolize a recent border dispute that the president was called upon to settle. So it was that on November 16, 1902, the first version of the now-famous "Drawing the Line in Mississippi" cartoon appeared in *The Washington Post.* Berryman drew a second version that set the standard for the bear (whom Roosevelt called "Berryman's bear," and whom Berryman called "Roosevelt's bear") that appeared in the artist's later cartoons about the president. As time passed, the little bear became a charming, respectful commentator on the president's activities, and it enjoyed widespread popularity among readers.

Just as Roosevelt had a gentle side to his nature, so did Berryman. While many political cartoonists took great pleasure in grotesque distortion of their subjects and seemed to delight in knifing them while tickling their readers' ribs, Berryman had a reputation for being a gentleman. As a result, his art and humor were filled with warmth and respect for his subjects. Perhaps, like Roosevelt, Berryman had a respect for the prey he hunted—one with a gun, the other with an artist's pen.

So, it would seem that the first seeds of the teddy bear legend were planted by two men guided by the gentler side of their natures.

While the teddy bear is considered a uniquely American concept, it could not have become such a popular toy without the help of a German toymaker named Margarete Steiff.

Stricken with polio as a girl, Margaret Steiff ignored her handicap and became first a successful dressmaker and later a successful toymaker. At the time President Roosevelt went on his famous hunting trip, Margarete Steiff was designing stuffed toys. The idea of making a jointed toy bear was suggested by her young nephew, Richard, who persuaded Margarete to

make one to show at the Leipzig Trade Fair in 1903.

Steiff's first jointed bear was not very popular with European toy buyers, but one enterprising American importer purchased 3,000 pieces. This order was then doubled and then increased again, so that by year's end, 12,000 jointed, stuffed bears had been shipped to America. By 1907, Steiff was sending more than a million bears to America.

About the same time that the first Steiff bears were making their American debut, the Ideal Toy Company's bear appeared on the scene. Although many collectors believe that Ideal created the first teddy bears, there is little evidence to support that claim.

The first recorded references to a toy bear being called teddy did not appear until some time later, in advertisements referring to "Teddy's bear."

By 1907, the little toy bear had taken the country by storm and children of all ages lined up to purchase one of their own.

So the teddy bear was born out of an act of kindness, nurtured by an artist's gentle wit, and fashioned by a physically handicapped toymaker to please her beloved nephew. Right from the start, the teddy bear represented the brightest side of human nature. Is it any wonder that over the decades, millions of us have embraced the kindly teddy bear, making him our constant companion and best friend?

♥

Why Do People Collect Teddy Bears?

Since the publication of my first book about teddy bears, *The TeddyBear Lovers Catalog*, in 1983, I have had the pleasure of being interviewed several times on television. Armed with my alterego and faithful companion bear, Hug, I fearlessly prepare for a series of probing, insightful, and possibly embarrassing questions about my personal relationship with my teddy bears. As you might expect, I'm often asked if I sleep with one or more of them.

Now anyone with any character would certainly refuse to name names, but I will confess that I do, in fact, sleep with my bear. And in this I am not alone. Millions of respectable adult humans take their bears to bed, finding solace and comfort in the warmth and friendship of a teddy bear.

Which brings me to the second most-asked interview question. "Why do people collect teddy bears?"

People who keep company with bears are often not really *collectors* but rather *lovers.* For there are thousands of humans who have just one perfect companion teddy whom they love.

True, there are many people who have vast dens of bears numbering in the hundreds and even thousands, but even these aficionados differ from the usual *collector.* Often the bears in these collections have no real monetary value as collectibles. Their charm is their ability to amuse and to create a sense of loving. It is equally true that there are many bears that have come to be valuable in terms of dollars, but whose intrinsic value still seems to be emotional.

It was Oscar Wilde who quipped that "nowadays people know the price of everything and the value of nothing." This remark led my bear, Hug, to reply, "Teddy bear: price on the ticket, value in the heart."

Today, there are over 5,000 bears in my den. Most are contemporary, handmade bears or mass-produced bears from Steiff, Gund, and other plush toy manufacturers. I still have many of my childhood bears who, like me, are more than fifty years old—hardly antique by any standard. There are several old bears that I rescued from the junkman and a few that have come to me for safekeeping after their original owners passed away. Their value to me is the loving sense of timeworn tradition I get as I watch them taking tea together on a balmy summer afternoon.

Hug says, "A teddy bear's virtue is that he cannot love himself. . .only others." And it is this spirit that seems to attract people to bears.

Why do humans crave soft, fuzzy bears as friends? Like most questions about love there is no easy answer. But perhaps, for so many of us, we form an unbreakable bond with our bears because a teddy was our first companion through the long and perilous journey from crib to maturity. Can't we all identify with Christopher Robin dragging a Pooh bear bump, bump, bump down the stairs?

♥

The Work of Teddy Bears

Giving bears to hospital patients has long been a tradition among teddy bear lovers. Many groups do this good work, but I guess the most famous is *Good Bears of the World*, which has bear dens worldwide.

Today, inspired by the good deeds of others, I bring bears to hospitals to work with terminally ill children. The children come from across the country for treatment; their parents and friends are often thousands of miles away. The bears and I do our best to make the kids a little happier. I tell stories, but the bears do the real work—they watch over the children at difficult times. In these kids' lives lurks a very real boogeyman, and the children all know that his name is Death. It's a big job for little bears, but they manage because they are filled with love—the love they're endowed with by children.

Sitting in a rocking chair with a six-year-old curled up in my lap, his bedraggled teddy clutched fiercely in his arms, I contemplate the wonder of our fuzzy friends. Soon, too soon, this sleeping child will go into surgery, and, if all goes well, a few months, even years, will be added to his short life.

I hold him closer; he reacts by clutching his bear even tighter. This is not my child—he is just one of many children that I work with, but tonight his parents have not arrived. Their plane is delayed, and I am filling in.

The child in my arms whimpers in his sleep as he struggles with some dark dream. His bear, called Pooper, gazes at him with alert eyes that promise both protection and unquestioning devotion. The child's dream passes and his breathing becomes even, but Pooper remains attentive, ever watchful.

I think about the times during my travels that I've awakened in the night in some strange hotel room, disoriented until I recognized one of my bears sitting nearby, like a sentry. It doesn't matter where I am; if there are teddies nearby, I know that I am safe.

Dawn stretches and casts a golden glow over the early morning sky. Outside, the city is coming alive as the prep nurses come in and take the child to surgery. One nurse carefully lifts the little boy out of my arms and gives Pooper to me for safekeeping. After they leave, I place him on the bed to wait for his friend's return.

"Keep your paws crossed," I tell him, and he looks at me, unblinking.

I stretch, swing my backpack of bears over my shoulder and head for the exit. In the hallway, an old gentleman shuffles along with a walker. As I pass beside him, he calls to me.

"You the teddy-man?" he asks in a voice that seems to shake his feeble frame. "The fellow with the bears?"

"Yes, I am."

"That's good work. Really helps, really does." His eyes brighten and his voice gets stronger. "I had a teddy but I gave him to my grandson. That bear helped me grow up, kept me company, made me laugh, and he really loved me. I gave him to my grandson so he could go on doing his job. Yes siree, givin' love, that's a bear's work."

He reaches out and takes my arm. "You wouldn't happen to have a little bear in there that might want to live in an old man's bathrobe pocket, I don't suppose?"

I swing the pack off my shoulder and rummage around inside until I feel a furry little critter just right for life in a pocket. I pull him out and hand him to my companion.

"Perfect!"

The old man looks around to see if anyone has observed our exchange and then shakes my hand and smiles. I start to leave once again when he calls after me.

"Don't feel silly."

I don't.

Outside, the morning air is clean and fresh, and I walk into the park for a moment alone. What a miracle life is, and how whimsical that in all their wonder and their pain, their confusion and their joy, human beings had the idea to create teddy bears to keep them company and help them make it through the hard times. I say my inner prayer for the safe passage of Pooper's young friend, and then I give special thanks for the imagination bestowed upon us to create such hardworking and magical creatures.

♥

How to Pick a Proper Teddy Bear

Having spent the better part of my life in the charming company of teddy bears, I feel that I can shed some light and a little expertise on the manner in which they are chosen. Actually, like kittens and puppies, teddies choose you by making themselves totally irresistible. You would assume that after the first couple of hundred they would all start to look alike, but on the contrary, they start to look even less alike. The more you see, the greater the differences.

When Madame Alexander, the renowned American doll designer, was asked if she had a favorite doll, she would slyly respond: "Does a mother have a favorite child?" A crafty answer. We all know that, in fact, mothers *do* have favorite children.

My first experience with teddy bear selection was in the presence of an English nanny. No, not *my* nanny, the other kid's. I had a grandmother. Standing side by side at the teddy bear counter at F.A.O. Schwartz, I brazenly eavesdropped as this haughty nanny described the proper bear to the saleslady.

"He must be sturdy," she began, "and his ears must be strongly sewn. He must be covered in the finest imported mohair, and his paw pads must be made of thick wool felt. He should be fully-jointed and, of course, be a Steiff."

On the last word, her nose lifted slightly as it probably did when she said the words Rolls-Royce or Tiffany. Her too-cleanly scrubbed, too-warmly dressed young charge looked bored. Bored and rich.

The clerk produced a fantastic golden-colored teddy bear wearing a bright red silk bow. She handed it gently to the nanny, who examined the bear thoroughly and proclaimed it satisfactory. It was boxed and delivered into the indifferent arms of my childhood counterpart.

Meanwhile, my grandmother had wedged her way behind the counter—self-service was her style—and was busily lining up candidates for adoption. She had a simple test for perfection: she hugged the bears. Stiff and unyielding ones would be replaced on the shelf. Stiff bears were, well, *too* proper.

After about twenty bears had made it into the semi-finals, Grandmother eased herself from behind the counter and addressed the clerk. "Excuse me, dear, but are there any more bears like these in the stock-room?" The clerk, naive enough to say yes, was dispatched to fetch them. My grandmother loved having bears fetched.

Eventually, there were about thirty bears in the finals. They had all passed the hug test and were now being interviewed. My grandmother peered intently into their jet-black, shoe-button eyes (which she said were the windows to their souls) and then repeated the hug test. At length she selected one or two that "spoke to her" and with whom she had "perfect rap-port."

By the time I was nine years old, I had mastered this technique of bear selection: in my best adult voice I would inquire if there were more bears in the stock-room, and, if there were, I'd ask the clerk to fetch them. In fact, I still do.

Teddy bears are often lifelong companions. Even those received as gifts soon become real friends that fulfill real needs.

Many people share their lives with only one bear, like a perfect husband or wife. Others have several bears that satisfy a variety of needs: a girl bear to go shopping with, a boy bear to watch the ball game with, or a tiny fellow to hide in a pocket for mutual comfort. And then there are people like me, who just can't get enough bears in their lives.

One of my best bear friends, Hug, says, "If beauty is in the eye of the beholder, every teddy bear will find a home." This is surely true. Some of the most beloved bears are the most bedraggled.

In teddy bear competitions, bears face off for big prizes in such categories as biggest, smallest, best-dressed, and so forth. But one category is not so easily judged. It's my favorite—Most-Loved Teddy Bear.

After judging perfectly-made and flawlessly-dressed bears for hours, it is refreshing to come to the Most-Loved group. Here one sees balding, patched, worn, and lovingly squeezed-thin bears. Their glass or shoe-button eyes are filled with the pride that comes from years of serving with honor as friends

and confidants. With their fur rubbed bald from loving hands, their ears resewn or replaced, their paw pads frayed and patched, they make me feel like a child again, seeking love, understanding, and security from a hostile and frightening adult world.

Looking into the eyes of the Most-Loved Teddy Bear contenders, I am smitten. But then I remember my grandmother—a real teddy bear expert—and all she taught me about love and how to choose a proper teddy bear. I give each tousled bear the definitive test—a hug. And the prize goes to that very special teddy bear that makes me feel most loved.

♥

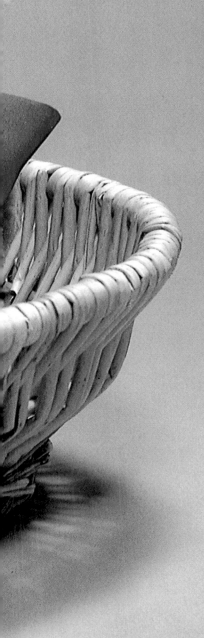

Are You Ready for Adoption?

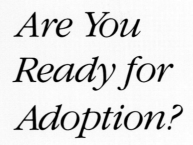

Living among teddy bears seems to bring out the storyteller in just about everyone. There are stories about the antics of humans and their bears and stories about the antics of bears and their humans. There are involved tales of lost bears and recovered bears, idyllic tales of enchantment, and occasionally even a yarn about a naughty bear (but these are quite rare).

One of my favorite teddy bear stories is about a little bear named Shrug.

As the last sweltering days of a New York summer were fading and the first hint of autumn was in the air, I headed uptown to my friend Steven's gift shop. I was in the mood for a new teddy bear, and his shop always had a good selection. The shop, situated in a swanky neighborhood just a few steps away from Beekman Place, catered to the gentry and contained fine china, expensive stationery and an array of tiny, ornate objects of no particular sort that served no particular purpose. One corner was devoted to expensive, imported toys and featured teddy bears.

Steven's shop always had a delightful fragrance of dried roses, and the window brimmed with promises that only money could keep.

Steven greeted me with a bright smile and a twinkle in his eye, telling me that a new batch of bears had arrived. Just as I was about to say hello to them, the shop door flew open and in whooshed a tall woman with a flamboyant sense of purpose. Her linen suit was straight from Fifth Avenue and some very unfortunate crocodile had provided her with matching handbag and shoes. Somewhere a hairdresser, a masseur, and a psychiatrist were probably adding wings to their summer houses, thanks to her checkbook. In one hand she carried a shopping bag from

Bloomingdale's, stuffed to capacity. In the other hand she carried a bright red-and-yellow Steiff box. She mumbled a condescending "excuse me" as she brushed me aside.

Her lack of what my grandmother called class revealed that this was a woman of recent money. She had probably married a man who was wealthy but not rich, and they probably had only part-time servants. I disliked her on sight, and being snubbed on the assumption that I was as unimportant as the china teapots she nearly shoved me into did little to endear her to me.

"I purchased this bear from you yesterday," she said, pushing the red-and-yellow box across the counter with the very tips of her fingers. She launched into her imperious oration without any salutation, which I suppose she felt was unnecessary since Steven was behind the counter and therefore a tradesperson.

"And," her voice raised to even loftier, more indignant tones, "it isn't perfect!"

She glared at Steven under lowered, turquoise painted eyelids, her crimson mouth held in a tight, prim expression.

Steven carefully opened the box and took out one of the golden-colored, twelve-inch tall, Margaret Strong teddy bears manufactured by Steiff. The bear's bright shoe-button eyes were close-set, and his stitched mouth held a hidden smile. In his innocence he believed that a human had loved him, adopted him, and taken him home forever. It is. after all, the nature of teddy bears to trust humans.

Steven examined the bear closely as the woman glared at him. Finally he asked what was wrong with the bear.

"Really," huffed the woman, "can't you see? One shoulder is higher than the other!"

Perhaps, I thought, he was only half shrugging. Frankly, being adopted by this woman was enough to make any bear shrug.

When Steven gets nervous, he stutters a bit. "Wha-wha-what do you want me to d-do about it?" he asked politely.

"What I want is a perfect bear!"

It was more of an imperial edict than a request. Steven disappeared into the stockroom, and I approached the woman as she stood drumming her fingertips on the countertop.

"Excuse me, madam, but do you have any children?"

"I beg your pardon," she snapped. I glared at her, my eyes demanding an answer. "Well, yes, as a matter of fact I do. Why?"

"Are they perfect?" I inquired.

"What? Perfect? Well, yes, of course they are." She hesitated and attempted a smile. "Well, you know, children are seldom really *perfect*."

"Did you return them when you discovered that they weren't perfect?" My eyes held hers and finally she looked aside.

"Of course not; don't be ridiculous. The very idea!" She regained her composure and huffed at me. "Indeed!"

Her glance attempted to dismiss me. It didn't work.

"Madam, that little bear thought you loved him, wanted him, and had adopted him forever. In that belief he trusted you, devoted himself to your happiness, and left here believing he had a new home. And now you want to return him because he isn't *perfect*."

I reached over and picked up the bear as Steven came back with an armload of fresh teddy bear stock. He lined them up and the woman, grateful to be away from me, grew absorbed in her search for a perfect bear. After looking them over and narrowing the field to three, she stepped back and sighed.

"This is awful. I can't decide, and none of these seems to have as sweet a face as the original one." She looked over at the original teddy who was nestled in the crook of my arm.

"I guess I'll keep the original one after all."

"Too late, madam; he doesn't want to live with you anymore. You abused his trust and broke his heart. He'll be happier with me." I turned and left the shop with my new bear.

Later that afternoon as Shrug and I were having honey-laced milk and ginger cookies, Steven called to say that the woman had waited for half an hour, thinking that I'd be back with the bear. Finally she had selected another bear. I couldn't help feeling sorry for the little fellow.

There's an old saying about being rich and being poor and how being rich is better. When a teddy bear calls your name and his eyes light up with the sight of you, *listen*. It will make you richer than you ever dreamed.

♥

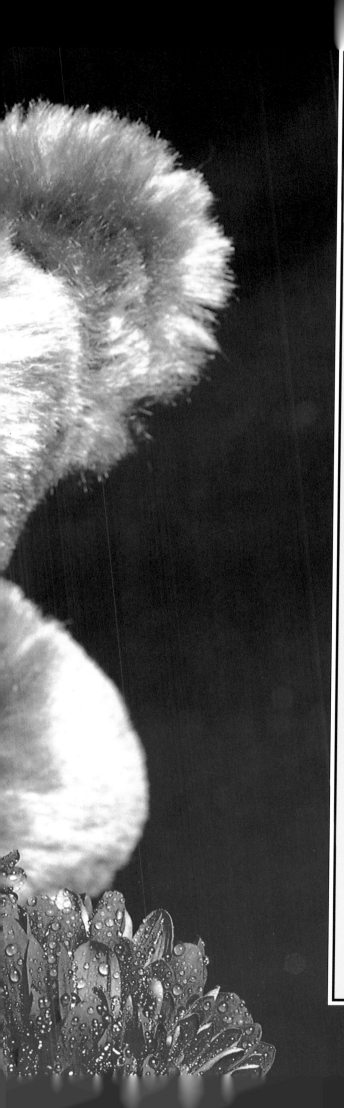

Bears in the Family Tree

How simple it all seemed when you adopted your first bear! There were only the two of you. You knew everything there was to know about him including when and where you found him, how much it cost to adopt him, and possibly even who made him.

But now, several years and dozens, maybe hundreds, of bears later—your memory is awash with mixed visions of bears and bear shops and manufacturers' names and dates and who *was* that tall, blond bearmaker you met in Seattle who sold you what's-his-name? You suddenly realize that your collection is a shambles of scattered sales slips and a jumble of hangtags. The bears all remember their names and who made them, but you can't document their value and now you want to insure them. You can't even remember where you adopted them.

Don't despair, listen to the Documentation Bear!

While it's enchanting to listen to one of your favorite bears rave about his great-uncle William the Unquenchable or his great-aunt Priss who once sat on Teddy Roosevelt's lap at a party in the Rose Garden, be warned: bears will go on at great length. The best way to organize your collection is to document your new bears as soon as they come home, when all the facts are fresh in your mind and easy to remember. Some bears have tags that tell you about them, but usually this is only a sketchy portrait and not enough for an insurance claim.

Begin by taking several color photographs of each teddy for a page in your documentation folio. The folio is simply a book or folder for storing photographs and papers for your bears.

Choose a closeup that captures all of teddy's facial charms—wistful glance, those enchanting eyes, and the cute nose. Then select a full-length photo that shows identifying physical characteristics: the long

arms and potbelly and turned-in toes. These photos will assist authorities if Teddy should wander off in search of honey and should need assistance in finding his way back home.

For each bear, fill out a documentation sheet, which will include the bear's name, vital statistics, and number.

I like to assign my bears a family number, which is like giving them their own Social Security numbers. The last two numerals are the year in which I adopted the bear. For example, a rather large brown bear named Humungous has the family number 500–7–87 which tells me that he is the 500th bear I adopted; the 7–87 tells me that the adoption was finalized in July. Write the bear's number on the back of each photo.

Even though you may have good pictures of your bear, it is wise to write out a good general description. Include details such as the sort of fur he has, and how tall he is. Measure him from top to toe (unless he is a sailor bear in which case you should measure him from stem to stern).

You might take note of any special features, such as whether or not he has a growler, if he is jointed or un-jointed, or if he's a yes-no bear.

Some collectors remove tags and buttons and such from their bears. Others want to preserve all the documentation that comes with the bear including all the hang tags. If you choose to remove the buttons and tags then file them with the bear's documentation sheet or in a file according to the bear's name and number. If possible, include the name and address of his maker in case you want to get in touch with them at a later date.

Personally, I hate paperwork and I put it off for as long as possible, making the task harder than it really is. Even though it may not be New Year's Eve, resolve to start documenting your bears today. When you're done, you can treat yourself and your bears to some milk and cookies.

♥

The Gentle Art of Sharing

My childhood was filled with wonder, and my generation may be the last to be rightfully called innocent. Born between the Great Depression and World War II, I saw many examples of how people celebrated their wins and coped with their losses: they shared.

Millions of Americans lost everything they owned in the Crash, but they survived by sharing what little they had with one another. That spirit helped them to survive the lean years. Still later, millions lost their lives in what was thought to be the war that would free the world forever. Time, and two subsequent wars, has shown us the folly of that innocent dream.

As an only child I was not required to share anything with brothers or sisters, neither my toys nor my parents' love. There were no children in my neighborhood to play with, so my teddy bears became my playmates. At times their world became more real to me than the world I lived in. They were my best friends and I cherished and protected them as they cherished and protected me.

When I was six or seven years old, I had to be hospitalized for one of those childhood ordeals such as tonsillitis. To help me get through it, I selected one of my many bears to accompany me.

At that age I had a great number of bears, due in part to the cleverness of adults who naturally feel compelled to give bears to young boys named Ted. While I had shared a great number of adventures with several of these furry friends, there was not one that had been worn to a frazzle by possessive love. So the bear that I brought with me to the hospital was in almost new condition.

In the bed next to mine was a boy about my age who seemed just about as frightened as I was. While he bravely discussed his impending surgery, he tightly clutched a very worn, very ragged teddy bear

named Buddy. I don't remember the name of my bear now, but George, my companion in the next bed, talked for hours about his great friend, Buddy, and all the experiences they had shared together. Buddy had been with him since the crib and had always gotten George through thunderstorms and scary nights.

Looking back now, I see that must have been an enormous job for one little bear. I had dozens of much bigger bears and the boogeyman still got to me every now and then. Maybe Buddy knew something that my bears didn't. Actually, I suspect Buddy knew more about love than my bears did, because George knew more about it than I.

George and I went into surgery early the following morning, and we both survived. We spent most of the afternoon eating ice cream and improvising sign language to communicate.

After dinner I became sick to my stomach and, as a result, my teddy bear had to be taken to the laundry, along with my pajamas. The experience left me both frightened and embarrassed. Feeling vulnerable without my teddy, I did the worst thing a boy could do—I cried.

In the bed across the room, George lay silently listening to my sobs. After a while he slipped quietly out of bed, came over to me, and placed Buddy beside me. Then he smiled and went back to his own bed. That's how I learned about sharing.

♥

The Astrological Teddy

The heavens have two constellations named for bears—Ursa Major and Ursa Minor—the big and little bears. So it seems fitting that teddy bears should look to the stars in search of their destiny. But casting a horoscope for your favorite bear may not be as easy as it might first seem. As any astrologer will tell you, the basis of a horoscope is the time of birth—not just the day, month, and year but the exact moment! But how can a bear determine the exact moment of his birth?

My inquiry led me to a very wise, very old bear who lived with an even older and wiser human astrologer. The bear, named Ursa Beara, and the astrologer, Madame Louisa, shared the secret of how to cast a perfect horoscope for a teddy bear.

"Since birth begins with life, or vice versa," explained Madame Louisa, "we set a standard for when a teddy first comes to life. That answer is remarkably simple . . . a teddy bear first comes to life in the heart of the person who loves him. So, a teddy is *born* the moment he is *loved*. Now, isn't that simple?"

Madame Louisa smiled as she refilled my teacup and put another honey cookie on Ursa Beara's plate. They seemed to nod at one another in perfect accord.

"Having determined that the first time you saw your teddy and loved him was . . . " Madame Louisa pressed a finger beside her nose and pondered for a moment, " . . . was, let us say—February the 4th, around 2:30 P.M., you would consult your charts and find that he is an Aquarian."

She lifted her teacup to her lips, brushed some cookie crumbs off Ursa Beara's chin, and continued.

"Human horoscopes are so very, very complicated since humans have many influences that alter and modify their personalities. Bears are more basic.

"While it is fairly clear that all bears born under the same sign are not alike, they are much more alike than humans born under that sign."

Ursa Beara told me much more about the differences and similarities of bears born under various signs, but her most telling remark was this: "No two bears are alike because no two humans are alike. And while it's true that all teddy bears love honey, *how* they love honey is determined by their zodiac sign."

Madame Louisa pulled her flowered shawl around her shoulders and gazed at her companion bear. The afternoon sunlight created a golden halo around Ursa's furry head, and her brown glass eyes sparkled.

"She's a very fine bear, very mystical and deep, but she's worthless in the kitchen," admitted Madame. "Can't even do dishes. She's a Scorpio and they hate doing dishes."

Ursa Beara seemed to smile and I sensed that they were a compatible pair. (Madame Louisa is a Cancer and loves homemaking.)

"The mysteries of the universe have been pondered since the dawn of time," mused Madame Louisa. "The Egyptians believed in the study of the stars, and since that time almost everyone has turned to the heavens in search of answers."

Astrologers, working with a system of star charts, determine the direction and movement of the stars and planets. They use this information to cast a personal star chart, called a horoscope. The art of astrology is the interpretation of the horoscope. Astrologers seldom read the same destiny from the same chart.

Ursa Beara commented that some people scoff at astrology and call it hocus-pocus. No matter. Astrology is still a great way to get to know your bear a little better.

♥

ARIES
The Ram
March 22 through April 20

The sign of the Warrior or Pioneer
Fire Sign
Ruler: Mars
Gems: Amethyst, Diamond
Color: Red • Metal: Copper
Compatible Signs: Sagittarius, Leo, Aquarius

The Aries bear has a tendency to fall in love quickly and ardently. Once this bear has fallen in love, he has great difficulty restraining his affection. In short, he is a born hugger!

This teddy bear, born under the sign of the Ram, is idealistic and imaginative as well as persuasive and demonstrative in relationships with humans. Gifted with a natural ability to make friends, the Aries bear has a charming tendency to give unexpected gifts to loved ones.

A natural problem-solver, he will not be daunted if the honey pot is stored on the topmost shelf. He will simply stack up boxes and chairs until he reaches his goal.

TAURUS
The Bull
April 21 through May 21

The sign of the Builder or Producer
Earth Sign
Ruler: Venus
Gems: Moss Agate, Sapphire
Colors: Blue and Pink • Metal: Copper
Compatible Signs: Capricorn, Virgo, Cancer

The Taurus bear can be affectionate and loving in his relationships with humans, but his tendency to think of his companion as exclusively his own can lead to fits of jealousy.

These bears, born under the sign of the Bull, can be determined, strong-willed, trustworthy, and practical. They have a strong desire to be surrounded with the luxuries of life and tend to overindulge in sweet cakes and honey.

The Taurus bear will stubbornly guard his honey and will often appear to pamper himself as he sits in an elegant chair and uses a silver spoon to devour the whole potful. But if you need some honey on a rainy day, this is the bear who will surely have it, for these teddy bears are always prepared.

CANCER
The Crab
June 23 through July 23

The sign of the Prophet or Teacher
Water Sign
Ruler: the Moon
Gems: Moss Agate, Emerald
Color: Green • Metal: Silver
Compatible Signs: Pisces, Scorpio, Taurus

The Cancer bear expresses love by creating a beautiful atmosphere in which to live. The teddy bear born under the sign of the Crab is a natural homemaker and would rather cuddle by the fire than go out on the town.

Tender and gentle with the younger bears, and parental regarding the fair distribution of honey, this sweetheart of a teddy is easily taken advantage of by a smooth-talking salesman.

Lavish with his affection, he is often cautious with money and a born bargain hunter. He will watch the household budget as though it was the national debt. And if there is a coupon for free honey, he'll find it faster than any other bear.

GEMINI
The Twins
May 22 through June 22

The sign of the Artist or Inventor
Air Sign
Ruler: Mercury
Gems: Beryl, Aquamarine
Color: Yellow • Metal: Quicksilver
Compatible Signs: Aquarius, Libra

The Gemini bear is too often flirtatious and irrepressible in the pursuit of pleasure.

Born under the sign of the Twins, these teddy bears often appear two-faced as they seem to be offering their honey with one hand while taking it back with the other. Delightful and amusing in conversation, they also have a real flair for writing.

When one of these bears falls in love, his affection is often charmingly expressed with little gifts and sudden, impulsive hugs. As the human companion of one of these bears, you will never be bored but often exhausted by this bear's ceaseless energy.

If you are short of coins and need a pot of honey, take this bear with you to the store and watch him con the owner with his smile.

LEO
The Lion
July 24 through August 23

The sign of the King or President
Fire Sign
Ruler: the Sun
Gems: Ruby, Diamond
Color: Orange • Metal: Gold
Compatible Signs: Sagittarius, Aries

The Leo bear often indulges in extravagant affection toward the one he loves, frequently putting the object of his affection on a pedestal.

The bear born under the sign of the Lion often sees himself as king of all he surveys. Magnanimous and generous, creative and a natural organizer, he can also be a bit of a tyrant. (Hide your honey, here comes the boss bear!) This bear has a sense of panache. If there are any red velvet ribbons lying around, he will find them and put them on. Dramatically inclined, he will often write, direct, and star in one of his own productions.

But be warned, never offer this fellow a discount brand of honey; he'll likely bite your head off!

VIRGO
The Virgin
August 24 through September 23

The sign of the Craftsman or Critic
Earth Sign
Ruler: Mercury
Gems: Pink Jasper, Sardonyx
Colors: Gray or Navy Blue • Metal: Quicksilver
Compatible Signs: Capricorn, Taurus, Pisces

The Virgo bear is often modest and discriminating in his choice of companions. In matters of the heart, the word fussy can often be applied. The honey must be pure and the datenut bread fresh.

The teddy bear born under the sign of the Virgin can, despite his elusive beauty, be a pain in the neck. This is a bear who will organize every trip down to the last minute detail and then want to waste hours taking a luxurious bath.

The Virgo bear has a marvelous sense of detail and is often creative to perfection. Ask this bear to make a shopping list and it will be neat and well-organized, but don't ask him to do the shopping himself . . . that could take all day.

SCORPIO
The Scorpion
October 24 through November 22

The sign of the Governor or Inspector
Water Sign
Ruler: Mars
Gems: Topaz, Malachite
Color: Deep Red • Metal: Iron
Compatible Signs: Cancer, Pisces

The Scorpio bear is full of passion and desire. To be loved by one of these fellows is like riding an emotional roller coaster. This is not a bear to be taken lightly!

The teddy bear born under the sign of the Scorpion has fire in his eyes and determination in his soul. Highly imaginative, discerning, and quick-witted, he will attempt to climb the highest mountain no matter the odds. That glow in his eyes will tell you that this guy is on the move, so watch out.

This bear will jealously guard his honey pot and hide it away; but just when you have decided that he is selfish, he will bring it out and share it with everyone.

LIBRA
The Balance
September 24 through October 23

The sign of the Statesman or Manager
Air Sign
Ruler: Venus
Gems: Diamond, Sapphire
Color: Indigo Blue • Metal: Copper
Compatible Signs: Aquarius, Gemini

The Libra bear all too often falls in love for the sake of being in love. Extravagant with his affection, this bear is easily hurt as his romantic idealism comes face to face with reality.

The bear born under the sign of the Balance or Scales is a born problem-solver. If two bears are having a dispute about whose honey pot is whose, set a Libra bear between them, for harmony is his middle name.

Often frivolous, discarding one bright bow for another, the Libra bear can be a devil of a flirt. Often sulking over imagined slights, this bear may be the first teddy to try to divorce you if you fail to give him sufficient hugs or keep the honey warm.

SAGITTARIUS
The Archer
November 23 through December 22

The sign of the Sage or Counselor
Fire Sign
Ruler: Jupiter
Gems: Topaz, Turquoise
Color: Purple • Metal: Tin
Compatible Signs: Aries, Leo

The Sagittarius bear is optimistic, jovial, and fun-loving where matters of love are concerned. This teddy bear is just plain fun to be around!

Generous to a fault, the bear born under the sign of the Archer is a straight shooter who is determined that everyone should have a good time. Red cars, bright stars, and Golden Blossom Honey for all is his motto. If you invite this teddy to a formal occasion he'll probably wear a tux and red sneakers.

Thoughtful, even intellectual, this bear loves good literature, especially if it involves mystery.

If you are sad, he'll do a somersault just to make you smile. This is a bear with a special pot of honey for every holiday—and every other day as well.

CAPRICORN
The Goat
December 23 through January 19

The sign of the Priest, Ambassador, or Scientist
Earth Sign
Ruler: Saturn
Gems: White Onyx, Moonstone
Color: Dark Green • Metal: Lead
Compatible Signs: Taurus, Virgo, Libra

The Capricorn bear is faithful and devoted, but often appears to be cool and standoffish. Modest and shy, this teddy bear, born under the sign of the Goat, is a perfect example of still waters that run deep. To be loved by one of these fellows is to be deeply adored.

Determined and disciplined, these bears are natural leaders and make wonderful generals. If you are organizing a teddy bear parade, this is the perfect bear to be the drum major. Often caught up in the latest fads in an attempt to be a trend-setter, the Capricorn is able to laugh at his own foolishness.

Give this teddy a task to perform and he will get it done lickety-split. As to the matter of honey, his brand will always be the very best.

PISCES
The Fish
February 20 through March 21

The sign of the Poet or Interpreter
Water Sign
Ruler: Neptune
Gems: Chrysolite, Moonstone, Bloodstone
Color: Sea-Green • Metal: Tin
Compatible Signs: Cancer, Scorpio, Virgo

The Pisces bear is totally ruled by his emotions in all of his relationships. Equally quick to smiles or tears, this teddy bear, born under the sign of the Fish, is sensitive, unworldly, and often impractical. He is, in a word, a dreamer.

Generous to a fault, hardworking and long-suffering, this bear is a front-runner in every humanitarian cause. All too often, this teddy bear seems bewildered and lost, incapable of running his life or finding his honey (which he probably donated to charity).

This bear's torrent of emotions is so deep and strong that he may appear to be torn apart by its intensity. But if there is ever a teddy bear saint, he will surely be a Pisces.

AQUARIUS
The Waterbearer
January 20 through February 19

The sign of the Truth-Seeker or Scientist
Air Sign
Ruler: Uranus
Gems: Sapphire, Amethyst
Color: Electric Blue • Metal: Uranium
Compatible Signs: Libra, Gemini, Aries

The Aquarius bear is the personification of loyalty. Kind and charitable, a bear born under the sign of the Waterbearer will do anything in the name of love.

Is there a good cause that needs a leader? He will take the helm. Are the smaller bears frightened of the thunder? He will gather them into his arms and sing to them. He can be high up on his favorite hill, watching a golden sunset, but one cry for help will bring him running to the rescue. This is a teddy with a giant heart.

Often this teddy bear can be unconventional, even eccentric, but he is simply asserting his personality, trying on a new attitude the way one tries on a new hat. And if you ask him to share his honey, he will warm it with his smile.

A Clean Teddy
Is a Happy Teddy

The ancient Romans built elaborate buildings to house their bathing pools. In those times bathing was a social event and a time when poets and philosophers exchanged ideas while luxuriously soaking. Today, hot tubs in the United States provide a shared bathing experience; in Sweden there is the sauna, and Japan has popular public bath houses.

Many historical figures, such as Cleopatra and Napoleon, enjoyed bathing rituals that included exotic perfumes and oils. During Hollywood's golden age, it was a tradition for movie stars to pose submerged in bubble baths. So it seems only natural that sooner or later, Teddy will find his way into the foam.

Unlike his childhood companions who loathe the Saturday night bathing tradition, Teddy actually enjoys having a bath. After all, he may get to bathe only a few times in his entire life.

Before you give your bear a bath, consider several things. First and foremost is his actual age or vintage. If he is a modern bear, manufactured of synthetic fur and filled with polyester, then he may want to jump into the washer-dryer with a bunch of big, fluffy towels and get dizzy in the spin cycle. To this teddy, the entire experience may seem like a roller coaster ride at Disneyland.

But if your bear is old and made of fine mohair or other natural fibers, he'll want a gentler bath, such as the sponge bath described below. While natural fibers and their blends may be washed and even dyed in their original form, they cannot be cleaned as easily once they have been made into a teddy bear. You should also consider Teddy's physical condition before deciding to wash him.

If your teddy is very old and has suffered considerable wear and tear over the years from hugging and loving, then you will want to repair him before his bath (or have him repaired by an expert).

Then there is the problem of . . . how can I phrase this gently . . . bugs! Ugh, these tiny little critters creep into Teddy's fur and nibble at his stuffing. These nasties must be gotten rid of before they eat up your bear or infest your entire den of bears.

Teddies who have been up in the attic too long or sitting on a shelf in the basement or garage are the most susceptible to infestation.

There are several ways to get rid of pesky bugs. Long storage in a cedar chest or a stay in a box filled with moth balls are effective forms of treatment, but these aren't much fun for Teddy, and they take too long.

A quicker, more effective way is to use a bug bomb. There are several brands on the market. (I use *Black Flag Formula S Automatic Room Fogger.* The twin-pack has two small cans and does the job nicely.) Use a small room or closet for average-size bears or a large cardboard box for tiny bears. Sit Teddy on some plain paper in the center of the space, and, following the product directions very carefully, spray him all over from a distance of about two feet. Don't spray him too much—just very lightly—but be sure you cover him all over. Then set down the bomb and leave Teddy alone in the room until the fogging is over. I usually do several bears at one time as it gives them some company during the purging process. Now Teddy is ready for his bath.

Here are a few items you'll need:
- brushes and combs
- fluffy terry cloth towels
- a soft brush or sponge
- a washcloth
- an electric hair dryer
- Woolite or similar mild soap

A special note about hairbrushes and combs: always use rubber combs (such as those made by Ace) and natural-bristle brushes that are soft as a baby's brush. Never, *never* use a comb or brush that has been used on human hair, because it will cause a static reaction with synthetic fibers. For the same reason, use separate combs and brushes for your synthetic-fiber bears and your natural-fiber bears.

A teddy bear is patient and long-suffering where chores are concerned; *you* must be as well. Pick a bright, sunny day and allow lots of time to get the job done. Whether your bear is antique or modern, the key word for all cleaning is *gentleness.* Always test teddy for colorfastness. Choose a small area on his

bottom or under his arm to test the washing solution and his color stability. There is always a bit of risk involved when giving a bear a bath, so besides gentleness, have patience and exercise caution.

Modern bears and vintage bears in good condition can easily be washed with a mild solution of Woolite or any pure, mild soap. Follow package directions carefully. Work the soap solution into foam and be sure to use only the foam for cleaning. Never get the water on your bear—only the foam!

Sit Teddy on a clean towel and, starting with the head, gently rub the foam into his fur with a sponge, soft brush, or washcloth. Do a small section at a time and avoid any soaking through to the stuffing. Avoid getting his nose and mouth threads wet, as these may not be colorfast. Never try to wash the felt paw pads and avoid getting them wet.

Remove the foam with a damp washcloth. Rinse out the washcloth and repeat until the foam has been completely removed.

If the bear is very dirty, you may want to repeat the process. Never scrub your bear—simply brush or wipe the foam with the washcloth. Repeat this process until the entire bear is clean. Always keep the rinse water clean. This will help you to see how much dirt is being removed.

After Teddy's bath, towel him damp-dry and sit him in the sun. Occasionally brush or comb him as he dries. You may also use a hair dryer on your bear, but be sure to use the warm or cool setting and keep the dryer about twelve inches away from the fur. Brush or comb the fur as you blow him dry. If his fur is long and has become snarled during the bath, use a comb with widely-spaced teeth to ease the snarls. Finish with a regular comb or brush. After Teddy has been bathed and brushed, he is ready for a bright new bow.

A final note about giving Teddy a bath: Today there are many handmade bears that are made of either synthetic or natural fibers. Since these seldom carry tags that identify their fabric or stuffing, ask the artist, or treat the bear as though he were a vintage teddy.

♥

When a Bow Is Not Enough

Teddy bears are beautiful no matter what they wear—or don't wear. The variety of their colors, furs, and faces is more than enough to distinguish one teddy from another, so dressing a bear to give him or her personality is a misconception. All teddies have personality; clothes simply *express* it!

If you're considering a new outfit for your bear, you should think *enhancement* rather than decoration. Even the simplest hat or ribbon may be all that's needed to express your bear's essence.

Most bears appreciate hats, sweaters, and jackets; lady bears love dresses. Since teddy bears enjoy life in general, and a jolly time in particular, what could be more fun for them than dressing up? Just as children like to pretend in Mother's bonnet and Dad's fedora, teddies like to indulge in new costumes of their own.

Generally, bears do a great deal of sitting about on beds and in chairs. When selecting an outfit, keep this in mind. Dresses that are open completely down the back are easier to sit in, and the skirt will flare out nicely. Pinafores and jumpers are especially attractive for this reason. If you're buying an outfit designed for a doll, the best styles are those created for infant or toddler dolls, as these tend to have high waistlines which are flattering to bears. Since bears usually have heavy arms and broad shoulders, be sure that the sleeves will fit. If your bear is a classic humpback type, this too, might cause a fitting problem.

Teddy bears have short legs and high waists, so choose fashions that either enhance this quality or disguise it. Trousers and coveralls are a particular problem and most ready-made pants will need to be shortened.

Much of the fun of dressing up teddy bears is the discovery of their versatility. Two fashion-conscious teddy bears who have distinguished themselves in the area of arctophile haute couture are Beau-Bear Brummel and Madame Coco of Paris, France, Europe. Their fashion know-how first appeared in *The Teddy Bear Lovers Catalog* and later in *BearHugs,* a monthly newsletter for teddy bears and their companions. Their reports, under the headline "When a Bow Is Not Enough," included not only the what but the why of fashion.

Once again they have consented to draw upon their vast experience and share a few bon mots from the fashion scene. Gallant as ever, Beau-Bear introduces Madame Coco as the first speaker. What follows is a transcript of their views. Madame Coco speaks:

"A lady is not (as some poets suggest) a work of art—which suggests a secondary form, that is, a thing created. Rather, a lady *is* art—a thing of beauty, forever a joy, and an object of admiration!

"A lady is elegant in the simplest of bows, especially bows of silk, velvet, or taffeta. Embroidered ribbons, so favored by French milliners, are best reserved for elegant hats where their exquisite designs can be fully appreciated.

"Since lady bears usually have lovely, luxurious fur, it seems a pity to obscure that natural beauty with too much costume. *N'est-ce pas?* Understatement, *mes chères,* is the very cornerstone of fashion. My namesake, the great Coco Chanel, is reputed to have said that in haute couture you pay for what has been *left off.* So, a hat with charming spring blossoms, and a bow, and accompanied by a sweet smile, may be quite enough to be stunning. Perhaps a charming enameled heart-shaped pin or a string of pearls might be used to accent the moment and express a mood. Lace shawls and collars, especially when held by an antique cameo pin, are also quite elegant.

"Now, if one is fortunate enough to have inherited a child's frock or an antique christening gown, I suggest that you reserve these for grand affairs, like Christmas or a birthday. Everyday fashion should be tasteful and simple. Imagination is the soul of fashion, and the clever teddy bear expresses herself with *panache* and *élan,* but never to excess.

"Still, there is room for the fully-gowned couture bear. With the recent publication of *Teddy's Bearzaar,* we saw how bears could look magnificent in gowns and jewels. These high-fashion teddies are at the zenith of couture and are created expressly to live in the spotlight. Theirs is a magical world—dressing by their own rules and dancing to their own music.

"However, a word to the wise: Avoid the foolishness of slavish devotion to a fashion which may not suit your own special *self.* Certain unfashionable bears, too overstuffed, overdressed, and haughty, their noses held high and their bearing too assumed to be real, might be advised to heed the incisive words of my Great Grandbear, Isadora (a bear of formidable splendor). She said: 'If you place yourself upon a pedestal, you would be well advised to remember that everyone standing below can look up your dress!' *Mon Dieu!*''

With a grandiose, sweeping gesture, Madame Coco turns the podium over to her distinguished and outspoken companion bear, Beau-Bear Brummel. He adjusts his brocade waistcoat, clears his throat, and speaks:

"Bare bears are boring! Get a tie. Get a scarf. Get a vest. Get dressed up!

"It seems to me that a gentleman should have a certain style and step out in his finest—be it designer jeans or a black silk top hat. Strut a little, show the world your stuff. Be bright, be bold, be colorful! Blah is boring!

"A gentleman bear might look his best in an old-fashioned, high, starched collar with a black silk bow tie and a snappy vest with an antique timepiece attached with a fine gold fob. A younger bear might prefer a brightly colored, hand-knit sweater, and a bear from the countryside might feel right at home in a pair of coveralls.

"Hats really are an expression of personality, and what bear is without personality? So, get a hat!

"The most important thing for the teddy bear, male or female, to remember about clothes is that they are intended to enhance—not obscure—your own special quality. Fashion should maximize—not minimize—personality and natural beauty. So get dressed up and have a fashionable day."

Beau-Bear Brummel and Madame Coco, we thank you for your contribution.

♥

A Matter of Manners

Is it considered polite to hug your teddy bear in public? Is it correct to introduce your bear first and then yourself? Should bears be allowed in the dining cars of Amtrak trains? These questions, and others just as compelling, are the special domain of America's most polite, most proper, most well-bred teddy bear, Ms. Etta-Ketta Bruin. Known on several continents as the Miss Manners of bears, she currently resides in a quiet corner of a posh teddy bear den where the afternoon sun filters through bamboo blinds and gives her fur a golden glow. Ms. Etta-Ketta Bruin has never married, but has been the hostess of numerous affairs. She has spread herself around, but not too generously to be considered gauche nor too sparingly as to appear cheap.

Looking at her fine mohair coat and pure glass eyes one feels that she was not merely *made,* but crafted out of some romantic Victorian fantasy. Truly to the manner born, she lives the quiet, genteel life once reserved for royalty and southern belles. She is said to have been a consultant on manners for *Gone With the Wind,* but that rumor is still unconfirmed. After all, a proper lady bear does not boast; she allows others to toot the horn for her accomplishments.

While the following notes on etiquette hardly cover the entire spectrum of possible situations involving bears and their human companions, it does present an attitude toward that special relationship between the two.

To this issue, Ms. Etta-Ketta Bruin speaks most knowledgeably and eloquently. What follows are a few of her maxims, which the astute reader would do well to take to heart.

• Politeness is a virtue, one of the few worth having. The lack of it certainly hampers one's climb up the social ladder.

• Never decline an invitation to an affair that involves either love or honey, as both are nourishment for the heart and spirit.

121

- Correct behavior is entirely based on whether or not it feels good, looks good, or tastes good. Remember that any discussion of good taste should be limited to its application to food.
- When traveling, humans should travel economy, with the luxury of two bears. The savings on the fare can be used to purchase quality honey.
- Eating in public is delightful if one is not too hungry. The distractions of conversation and passing strangers require one to divert one's attention from the meal.
- Speaking of strangers, never agree to dine with perfect strangers. They are seldom perfect and usually stranger than you'd care for.
- As to the question of proper introductions between bears and humans, I have come to this logical conclusion: Since the humans in question probably have little in common besides their appreciation of teddy bears (which is more than sufficient), it seems only fitting *and* proper that they introduce their bears first and then themselves.
- Should you hug your teddy bear in public? Of course you should! Don't you want other humans to know how lovable you are? Don't you want them to see that you are the companion of a perfectly delightful teddy bear? After all, a little envy is good for the soul. Isn't it?
- It is my feeling that teddy bears and their human companions should openly cavort together, especially at picnics and by the seashore. I think that they should sail together, fly together, train together and—while I prefer not to take them myself—bus together.
- The love and affection between human and teddy has a long tradition going back to the father of us all, Teddy Roosevelt. Humans without a teddy bear to love and be loved by are adrift in a sea of loneliness. Pity them, show them the way—buy them a bear!

As the sun's last rays illuminate the corner of the room where she sits, Ms. Etta-Ketta Bruin rings for tea. Like a perfect lady, she pours the steaming brew which has been generously laced with fine, imported honey.

She passes the tea and the honey cookies, but not until she has served herself, and when I bring to her attention this rather obvious breach of etiquette, she archly replies:

"You are, of course, referring to human etiquette, which is, as I have already pointed out, not based on any teddy bear lore. The fact of the matter is that honey and happiness take priority over everything, including manners. So, if you please, pass the cookies!"

♥

The Traveling Teddy

Basically, teddy bears travel in one of two ways: with or without their humans. The rules of the road vary accordingly. Nowadays, many humans and bears travel together, visiting other arctophilists at shows and conventions. Bears in the company of humans have a fairly easy time of it because their human will usually do all the hard work, and Teddy can sit back and enjoy the ride. Often, bears who travel by air enjoy the same pleasures as children. If you ask politely, the flight attendant may give your bear some flight wings or other pins and buttons.

However, both Teddy and his friend should take a few things into consideration when traveling. When you take your teddy abroad, unless you are a small child or a white-haired granny, some customs inspectors may suspect that Teddy has something to hide (like the Pharaoh's jewels). One poor bear had all his stuffing yanked out at the Egyptian border, and his poor human was so upset that she took the next flight home. Usually such things don't happen, but a smart bear should demand an x ray before any surgery is performed. If you're carrying your teddy in a flight bag that will ride through an x-ray machine, you might explain that the object in his tummy is only his voice box.

One of my favorite traveling companions is a four-inch tall bear who rides in my pocket. He is a Steiff from about 1907 who originally belonged to my grandfather, and I call him Grandpa.

On a flight back from a recent convention, we experienced some turbulence caused by a thunderstorm. I reached into my pocket and stroked Grandpa to reassure him that I was keeping one eye on the plane's wings to be sure that they hadn't fallen off. Across the aisle, a frightened-looking child was clutching her mother. Her mother was talking softly to her, but the child couldn't hear anything but the sound of her own fear. I reached into my pocket and brought out Grandpa.

"Time to go to work, old man," I whispered as I

handed him over to the scared child. Immediately she smiled and was busily examining him as the plane maneuvered through the storm. Neither she nor Grandpa even noticed that the wings hadn't fallen off.

The second type of traveling teddy is the one who goes solo. Since many humans can't afford extensive travel, they send their bears instead. Human pen pals, separated by miles or oceans, find that they feel closer to one another if they exchange bears. These bears are not gifts, but guests, and are subject to certain rules of etiquette.

If an invitation to visit has not been forthcoming then a polite request should be made in advance. Surprise visits are not always a pleasure, and Teddy risks the possibility of being left like a foundling on the doorstep. So write or phone ahead.

Many bears keep a travel journal or a souvenir bag. The polite teddy will not be too demanding of his host to make entries in the journal or to fill the goodie bag to the brim.

A wise bear carries a small amount of mad money in case he sees an expensive memento for his human, or if he wishes to be photographed at the local hot spots. Some bears have their own cameras and extra film for such occasions. And, of course, it is always good form to provide one's own return fare home.

Teddy's travel case or carton should be sturdy enough to make the round trip and be roomy enough for any extra goodies acquired during the visit. The very social teddy bear who has several pen pals may want to bring along several stamped, addressed envelopes to send notes to buddies around the country or overseas.

Before sending Teddy off on a visit, discuss how a guest should behave, and explain that when it is time to go home, it is impolite to hang onto the banister or hide under the bed. A polite teddy gets invited back another time.

A note of caution: Remember poor Paddington—he ended up lost in a vast train station with only a tag pinned to his coat asking that he be looked after. Not all bears are as lucky as he was in finding a new family. Be sure that your bear traveler carries proper ID, and be sure to tuck a note in one pocket with your address and phone number on it.

As traveling companion or houseguest, a teddy bear will always make the day a little brighter.

♥

The Question of Value

While not everyone who keeps company with a teddy bear considers him- or herself a collector, some arctophiles are collectors in the strictest sense. Armed with the latest price guide, these anxious buyers are ever watchful for the bargain bear, in the hopes of turning a profit. Stories abound of antique bears making their way around a show in a matter of hours and increasing in price as they move from dealer to dealer even before the show opens to the public. But the operative word here is price—not value.

Value, like beauty, may be entirely in the eyes of the beholder. Most of the teddy bear collectors I know buy their bears for pleasure and not for resale. But that doesn't mean that teddy bears aren't good investments.

Some bears will increase in price simply by getting older as they sit in the attic. These have what might be called second-generation resale increase. The other kind of collectible bears, what might be called an early-maturing market, is represented by limited production, numbered series, one-of-a-kind pieces, and artist-signed teddy bears. Recently, manufacturers have produced a number of these bears.

In some cases, the original limited edition sold out quickly, a secondary market followed hot on its heels, but then sales bottomed out in the third generation, making it difficult for the third buyers to sell the bears profitably. Some special edition teddies never even sell out their original production.

How can you tell which bears will bring you a return on your money? I've developed the following list of criteria to determine whether a bear is likely to increase or hold its worth in the marketplace.

• *Beauty, quality, and originality.* These three qualities require no explanation. They are the cornerstone of virtually every collectible.

• *Popularity.* Bears made by Steiff, for example, have stood the test of time and are definitely col-

138

lectible. The occasional trendy or instantly popular products, like the Cabbage Patch Kids dolls, may also be secure investments. Because of their current success, they stand a good chance of becoming collectibles in the future, in the same way that Superman comics and Davy Crocket coonskin caps are prized today.

Products based on popular characters, such as Winnie-the-Pooh, Paddington, or any of the Walt Disney characters are also worth collecting.

• *Unpopularity.* Most discontinued items become valuable on the secondary market. These bears are harder to identify in their own time. They may be rediscovered when tastes change.

It's true that a less popular item means limited production and less availability, but be advised—something scarce is valuable only if people are looking for it. Hen's teeth are supposed to be scarce, but who's looking?

• *Innovation.* New advances in teddy bears, such as Teddy Ruxpin and all the other electronic talking bears, may be a sign that these bears could become the collectibles of the future. But then, maybe not!

• *Artistry.* This is the most difficult area of all in which to speculate. Although I am a dedicated supporter of teddy bear artists and their work (after all, I make bears myself), it is nearly impossible to predict what secondary market may exist for these bears.

One has only to look at the history of the fine art market to see how many gifted artists starved for money and attention in their own lifetimes. Hopefully, this will not be the fate of today's teddy bear artists.

Just as the early work of many painters is less respected than their later work, the early work of bear artists may be less revered than their current output. But what constitutes "early work," and at what point is the work "mature" or even "late"? There are teddy bear artists whose entire output may number only several dozen pieces. Some artists can make a bear in a matter of hours; others spend weeks of painstaking labor.

Collecting for the fun of it is one of life's greatest joys, but collecting for profit may become a giant headache. Perhaps you can have it both ways if you remember that a thing of beauty is a joy forever—and possibly a thing of value as well. My best advice is to buy only the bears *you* like, regardless of investment potential.

♥

Hunting Bear

When I became a serious collector of teddy bears (as opposed to one who only occasionally fell prey to the wiles of a charming teddy), my search led me down every possible avenue: I awoke before sunrise to be first in line at antique shows and flea markets; I flew across America, gathering up armloads of handmade art bears available at special teddy bear gatherings; I melted my Visa and MasterCard at the registers of teddy bear shops all along the California coast; I drove to rural areas searching for old bears and new bears handcrafted by artisans living deep in the woodlands, who carved bears from local trees or fashioned them from homespun yarns.

Now, several years and thousands of bears later, I feel that the search has just begun. Rumors of handmade bears from Africa make my heart pound, and the promise of bears from Australia gives me a rush that once only chocolate could induce.

When I began my quest, I was overwhelmed to discover that there were hundreds of stores across America dedicated to the art of teddy bears. Imagine my delight at discovering that in the ensuing years an additional hundred or more have opened. While a store devoted entirely to teddy bears is certainly a spectacular place to find a furry friend, it is by no means the only source. Many people prefer hunting bears in mail-order catalogs. There are, of course, many pitfalls to mail-order shopping, not the least of which is the waiting time. Frankly, I shop every way available, and when a mail-order bear finally does arrive, it's a delightful surprise.

Many shops advertise in the teddy bear publications and offer shopping by mail. These shops also stock limited-edition bears made for them, which are prized by collectors.

For me, the best possible way to find new bears is to attend a teddy bear event. Bear aficionados have concocted every possible reason to gather, from tea parties to picnics to full-scale conventions and rallies.

These events may last anywhere from a few hours to several days, but they are all memorable, fun-filled, and wallet-depleting experiences. The following is a sampling of some better-known, annual events—but this is merely the tip of the iceberg since it seems that there is some sort of teddy bear event every week of the year.

In California, the homeland of teddy bear artists and the hotbed of collectors, there are so many shows (but never *too* many!) that listing them would be next to impossible. However, one event is especially significant for its historical value. In the charming community of Los Gatos, California, stands America's *first* teddy bear store, *Bears In The Wood*. Every year, the store celebrates Teddy Roosevelt's birthday (October 27). Visiting this wonderful shop any day of the year is an event; this celebration day makes the experience that much better.

Several large teddy bear clubs in northern and southern California sponsor events for their members and for the general public. The *Northern California Teddy Bear Boosters* meet in the San Francisco area, and once a year a group of southern California clubs join together as the *International League of Teddy Bear Clubs* and stage a convention and sale that attracts artists and collectors from across the country.

In Minneapolis, *The Teddy Tribune*, America's number one arctophile newspaper, hosts an annual four-day convention that is unsurpassed.

During the summer months rallies, shows, and conventions are held in Seattle, Houston, Chicago, San Diego, Baltimore, and Amherst, to name just a few. Most events are listed in the various teddy bear publications as well as most of the newspapers devoted to antiques and collectibles. When there is no nearby show or sale, there's always a flea market, a church bazaar, or a local yard sale to satisfy the hunger for bear.

To a true hunter, no game is too elusive, no distance too great, and no hurdle too high in the quest for that certain bear.

♥

The Well-Crafted Teddy Bear

In just a few years, the beloved toy companion of millions of children has evolved from a plaything to a work of art. The creators of teddy bear art are following in the footsteps of every artist that has preceded them through the ages. When an artist first puts pencil to paper or when the teddy bear maker first designs a pattern, the goal is to create something special, personal, and unique. The act of creating is satisfying in itself and, for a period of time, it is simply enough for the artist to engage in the work without any other reward.

Then a friend stops by and says what a wonderful thing it is that was created, and the element of response enters into the equation. The next time the artist puts pencil to paper, a part of him or her hopes that the drawing will not only satisfy the urge to create, but also evoke a positive response from someone else.

When at last the artist sells the work, a third element is added to the equation. Now when the artist sits down to create, he or she hopes that the work will satisfy all three criteria: creativity, response, and reward.

Any one or all three of these elements may add up to a feeling of success. Each artist is different. For some, simply creating is a measure of success; for others, it is the public's response; and for still others, it's the cash sale that says it was worth the effort.

Like any artist, the teddy bear maker has dreams: the dream of creating the perfect bear; the dream of winning a blue ribbon in competition with his or her peers; the dream of being recognized in a publication; or the dream of being successful financially.

As the teddy bear community becomes closer and the artists mix business with pleasure, traveling around the country to a variety of shows, a new kind of unity is developing. There's a new sense of cooperation to achieve similar objectives.

Recognized artists conduct workshops, sharing experience and knowledge with novice bear makers. When a show opens to the public, everyone understands that each individual contribution is responsible for making the show a hit, giving the audience its money's worth so that people will come back next year.

The teddy bear artists have become a bit like a traveling circus troupe, going from city to city, setting up in the early morning light, shouting greetings to fellow artists, borrowing tape, sharing a Danish and a bit of gossip while working toward that moment when the door opens and the show begins. Afterward, when the show is over, the artists gather together again, swap stories and compare notes. They pack up, weary from the intensity of the day, and, amid shouts of "See you in Chicago," they head off into the night.

Teddy bear artists have achieved a nationwide sense of solidarity in just a few years. Five years ago, only those artists within traveling distance of each other had any communication with others working in the medium of teddy bear art. Then, as more and more conventions and shows featured their work, and with the formation of the American Teddy Bear Artists Guild (ATBAG), the artists began to gather and become comrades. Networking began, and information—from new sources of fabric to which shows were the best to attend—was passed around the country. Within just three years a functioning community had developed.

One standard of excellence in the world of art has always been the exhibition of work by museums and galleries. There, in the rarified atmosphere of vaulted ceilings and perfect lighting, works of art are presented in a manner that enhances and validates their existence. Each piece sits on its own pedestal, perfectly posed, expertly lit, waiting to be viewed, commanding respect.

On September 21, 1987, the teddy bear artist community achieved a goal that many artists never reach. That evening, amid colorful balloons, ribbons, and fanfare, the doors of the Incorporated Gallery on Madison Avenue in New York City opened on the first exhibition by teddy bear artists. Within minutes, the first bear was sold for $1,500, and a kind of art history was made. The teddy bear maker had become a recognized, legitimate, and economically viable *artist*.

During the course of the exhibit, hundreds of people came to see the bears. Elegant art buyers stepped from their limos and mingled with curious collectors and delighted schoolchildren who had never seen bears as wondrous as these. Everyone reacted with childlike delight as the bears struck their poses, radiating whimsy and charm. By every standard, the gallery show was a complete success.

Today, teddy bear artists are creating even more exciting, gallery-quality pieces that command gallery prices. Even commercial companies have taken notice and have begun to hire teddy bear artists to create expensive signature lines of bears.

Every one of the teddy bears in this book was created by a successful, working teddy bear artist. Each bear is a work of art, an expression of creativity. But more than that, each bear is an expression of joy, wonder, and love.

♥

For Your Information

All of the bears shown in *The Teddy Bear Lover's Companion* are original designs and are protected by copyright in the artist's name.

1 Barbara Sixby
2 Rosalie Frischmann
4 Flore Emory
5 Genie Buttitta
7 Ted Menten
8 Corla Cubillas
9 Flore Emory
10 Kathy & Owen Sandusky
12 Suzanne De Pee
13 Hillary Hulen
14 Catherine Bordi
16 Candy Corvari
17 Ted Menten
20 Carolyn Jacobsen
22 Denise Dewire
23 Ted Menten
24 Barbara Sixby
27 Tracey Roe
29 Ann Cranshaw
30 Julie Zano
31 Steve Schutt
33 Cindy Martin
35 Jane Carlson
37 Joyce Francies
38 Diane Gard
39 Flore Emory
40 Barbara Wiltrout
43 Tracey Roe
44 Steve Schutt
46 Diane Gard
47 Diane Gard
48 Linda Spiegel
51 Carol Cavallaro
52 Linda Spiegel
53 Cathie Levy
54 Ted Menten
56 Judi Maddigan
58 Diane Sherman
59 Cathie Levy
60 Suzanne Marks
63 Carol Cavallaro

64 Althea Leistikow
66 Lynda Buckner
67 Flore Emory
68 Candy Corvari
69 Cindy Martin
70 Judy Hill
73 Carol-Lynn Rössel Waugh
74 Kathy & Owen Sandusky
76 Deanna Brittsan
77 Genie Buttitta
78 Kimberly Hunt
80 Suzanne De Pee
82 Carolyn Jacobsen
83 Shirley Howey
84 Diane Gard
86 Ann Inman
88 Kathy Mullin
89 Mary Holstad
90 Kathy Mullin
91 Beverly Port
92 Brenda Dewey
94 *top:* Kathy & Owen Sandusky
94 *bottom:* Linda Suzanne Shum
95 *top:* Judy Hill
95 *bottom:* Patricia Blair
96 *top:* Cindy Martin
96 *bottom:* Barbara Sixby
97 *top:* Judy Hill
97 *bottom:* Kimberly Hunt
98 *top:* Suzanne Marks
98 *bottom:* Celia Baham
99 *top:* Lauri Sasaki
99 *bottom:* Linda Spiegel
100 Joanne C. Mitchell
101 Genie Buttitta
102 Candy Corvari
105 Ted Menten
107 Lynda Buckner
108 Tatum Egelin
109 Doris & Terry Michaud
110 Marcia Sibol
113 Diane Gard
114 Ted Menten
115 Ted Menten
116 Ted Menten
117 Marcia Sibol
118 Tammie Lawrence

119 Corla Cubillas
120 Gloria Rosenbaum
122 Ann Inman
124 Kathy & Owen Sandusky
125 Beverly Port
126 Barbara Conley
127 Ted Menten
128 Charlotte Joynt
130 Cindy Martin
132 Lauri Sasaki
133 Flore Emory
134 Barbara Whisnant
135 Althea Leistikow
136 Carol-Lynn Rössel Waugh
138 Jacquelyn L. Allen
140 Steve Schutt
141 Wendy Lockwood
142 Ted Menten
143 Brenda Dewey
144 Lynn Lumley
146 Marcia Sibol
147 Marcia Sibol
148 Sue Newlin
151 Deanna Brittsan
153 Kimberly Hunt
154 Heather De Pee
155 Kathy Mullin
156 Diane Gard
158 Steve Schutt
159 Corla Cubillas
160 Barbara Conley
Front Cover Ted Menten
Back Cover Ted Menten

Publications

The Teddy Tribune
254 West Sidney Street
St. Paul, Minnesota 55107

Teddy Bear and Friends
900 Frederick Street
Cumberland, Maryland 21502

Teddy Bear Review
170 Fifth Avenue
New York, New York 10010

♥